SAN FRANCISCO

BY DEBORAH KENT

CHILDREN'S PRESS®
A Division of Grolier Publishing
New York London Hong Kong Sydney
Danbury, Connecticut

CONSULTANTS

Marlene Smith-Baranzini
Associate Editor of *California History,*
the quarterly journal of the California Historical Society
Coauthor of USKids History series

Linda Cornwell
Learning Resource Consultant
Indiana Department of Education

Project Editor: Downing Publishing Services
Design Director: Karen Kohn & Associates, Ltd.
Photo Researcher: Jan Izzo

Library of Congress Cataloging-in-Publication Data

Kent, Deborah.
     San Francisco / by Deborah Kent.
       p.   cm. — (Cities of the world)
     Includes bibliographical references and index.
     Summary: Describes the history, culture, people, daily life, and points of
interest of this beautiful city on San Francisco Bay.
     ISBN 0-516-20466-1 (lib.bdg.)   0-516-26241-6 (pbk.)
     1. San Francisco (Calif.) — Juvenile literature.   I. Title.
II. Series: Cities of the world (New York, N.Y.)
F869.S34K46   1997   96-54706
979.4'61—dc21   CIP
                                     AC

TABLE OF CONTENTS

BE BUILT

On summer mornings, fog rolls into San Francisco Bay from the Pacific Ocean. Softly it folds over the Golden Gate Bridge, wrapping it like a veil. The bridge arches over the Golden Gate, the narrow channel between the bay and the sea. It extends a graceful welcome to oceangoing ships as they steam into port. For seafarers, the bridge is the first glimpse of San Francisco, California.

The Golden Gate Bridge hangs between tall towers planted at either end. It swings in strong winds much as a spider's web swings between two fence posts. From a distance, the bridge looks lacy and fragile. Yet it bears six lanes of thunderous traffic day and night. The suspension cables that appear so delicate from far away are actually 3 feet (0.9 meter) in diameter. Each cable is made up of 27,000 twisted strands of wire.

When work began on the Golden Gate Bridge in 1933, many people said it couldn't be built. At 8,981 feet (2,737 m), it would be one of the longest suspension bridges in the world. Even if it were finished, opponents warned, it would sway to pieces in the high winds that sweep across the bay. If the winds didn't tear it down, it would collapse in the next earthquake.

Boats sailing under the Golden Gate Bridge, one of the longest suspension bridges in the world

*Left: The Golden
Gate Bridge at sunset*

*Below: A young
Asian American San
Francisco resident*

The Golden Gate Bridge defied these gloomy predictions. Since it opened in 1937, it has withstood lashing storms and a major earthquake. When people think of San Francisco, the Golden Gate Bridge is often the first image that springs to mind. With its exquisite beauty, it is a fitting symbol of this lovely city on the bay.

In another important way, the Golden Gate Bridge captures the spirit of the city. It is strong and persistent, holding out against the elements. The people of San Francisco have endured hardships, too. After earthquakes and fires, they have rebuilt their city and their lives. Like the bridge they love, San Franciscans are stubborn survivors.

Leaving their homes and villages they crossed the ocean only to endure confinement in these barracks. Conquering frontiers and barriers they pioneered a new life by the Golden Gate.

—Inscription on a monument at the former immigration station on San Francisco's Angel Island

GATEWAY TO THE WORLD

In 1848, gold was discovered in the California hills 100 miles (161 kilometers) from San Francisco. From all over the world, people poured into the city. The newcomers were shocked by San Francisco's cost of living. Tiny houses rented for $800 a month. Eggs sold for $1 apiece. Despite the outlandish prices, more and more people flocked to the city. San Francisco was the gateway to the golden west.

San Francisco is still one of the most expensive cities in the United States. Rents are among the highest in the country. Jobs can be hard to find. Yet the city continues to draw newcomers from across the country and around the world. Today, it is home to more than 700,000 people. They come for the beauty of its hills and beaches. They are lured by its art and music. They come to enjoy the charm of its neighborhoods. Somehow, the pleasure of living in San Francisco is worth the high prices.

On a map, San Francisco looks like a fist at the end of a long arm of land. The arm is a peninsula. It is washed on the west by the Pacific Ocean and on the east by San Francisco Bay. Because San Francisco has always been a major seaport, it has long attracted people from every country in the world.

The faces of the children in these pictures reflect the fact that San Franciscans come from countries all over the world.

Today, official school notices are sent home in Chinese, Japanese, Spanish, Italian, and Tagalog (the chief language of the Philippines), as well as in English. San Francisco is a city of many faces.

The earliest inhabitants of the San Francisco Bay area were small tribes of Native Americans. Today, these different tribes are often grouped together and called the Mission Indians. Descendants of the Mission Indians, as well as people of many other Pacific Coast tribes, still live in San Francisco today.

The first Europeans to reach present-day San Francisco were sailors who came from Spain in the 1540s. They were followed in the 1770s by Roman Catholic missionaries who wanted to convert the Indians to Christianity. Their first church, Mission Dolores, still stands today. The surrounding Mission District is the heart of San Francisco's Spanish-speaking community. Most Hispanics in San Francisco are of Mexican heritage. Markets in the Mission District sell strings of garlic and dried peppers. Girls celebrate their fifteenth birthdays with the traditional *quincenera* party. Dozens of friends and relatives gather for live music, dancing, and mountains of food.

Strings of dried peppers like this are sold in Mission District markets.

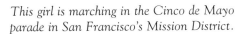
This girl is marching in the Cinco de Mayo parade in San Francisco's Mission District.

A tiled gate decorated with dragons welcomes visitors to San Francisco's Chinatown. San Francisco has a larger Chinese population than any other American city. In fact, there are more Chinese people in San Francisco than anywhere else outside of Asia.

Beyond the arch, Chinatown is a world apart. Signs are printed in Chinese characters instead of English letters. Phone booths on the street look like miniature Chinese pagodas. Dragons curl around pillars and lamp posts. Tiny shops offer powdered herbs and dried snakes. These ingredients are used in traditional Chinese medicines.

To outsiders, Chinatown is best known for its restaurants. Diners feast on such delights as steamed dumplings, pork in sweet and sour sauce, and chicken with cashews. For dessert there are always fortune cookies—an American creation.

Above: Fortune cookies are always offered at the end of a meal in Chinatown.

Left: Asian men relaxing in a Chinatown pavilion

The high point of life in Chinatown is the Chinese New Year. According to the Chinese calendar, the new year begins on the night of the first new moon between January 20 and February 20. The holiday is a week-long extravaganza of fireworks, pageants, and elaborate family parties. The grand finale is a spectacular parade with gongs, bands, and floats.

Costumed girls at a Chinese New Year celebration

The Living Dragon

During the Chinese New Year parade, children crowd the sidewalks to see the living dragon. The dragon stretches about 150 feet (46 m), nearly twice as long as any dinosaur that ever walked the earth. Some 50 people inside the gigantic costume make the dragon twist and coil its way through the streets. Lanterns give the creature an eerie glow from within.

Most of the houses in San Francisco's Japantown have carefully tended gardens. Here and there, a tiny bonsai tree sprouts. Following ancient practices, bonsai trees are trimmed and shaped so that they remain small. Every April, Japantown, or *Nihonmashi*, celebrates its annual Cherry Blossom Festival. Families gather in the parks for picnics. The children run and play tag. Grown-ups admire the snowy white flowers that cover the cherry trees.

Right: Two Japanese boys giggling and acting silly

Below: Participants in Japantown's annual Cherry Blossom Festival

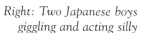

Many other ethnic groups are well represented in San Francisco. The African American community is centered in the Fillmore District. This neighborhood developed when black people came to the city from the South after World War II. The city's Little Italy section preserves the customs of Sicily and of northern Italy. Here and there, San Francisco has enclaves of Filipinos, Germans, Russians, Irish, and other nationalities.

Many houses in San Francisco's most expensive neighborhoods date back to the 1800s. These colorfully painted Victorian-style houses have ornate decorations and balustrades. They are often called "painted ladies." Homes in Pacific Heights are shielded from view by high prickly hedges. Many have balconies and pillared porches.

Tragically, San Francisco also has pockets of terrible poverty. Perhaps the most notorious is the Tenderloin District. This is the refuge of many of the city's homeless men and women. The streets of the Tenderloin are lined with bars and cheap hotels called flophouses.

Whatever neighborhood they live in, San Franciscans are constantly on the move. Getting from place to place in San Francisco presents unique challenges and pleasures.

Rooflines and architectural details of some of San Francisco's famous "painted ladies"

A CITY OF UPS AND DOWNS

San Francisco's Lombard Street is called the "crookedest street in the world." In a single block, it makes eight hairpin bends. Lombard is a one-way street. All its traffic flows downhill. A driver who misses a turn is likely to crash through someone's living-room window.

The streets of San Francisco climb up and down some 43 hills. Parked cars and trucks sometimes start to roll, causing major pileups. "Prevent runaways!" warn signs at the parking meters. "Curb wheels. Park in gear. Set brake." In places, the hills are so steep that steps are built into the sidewalks. San Franciscans like to joke, "If you get tired of walking around this city, you can always lean on it."

One day in 1869, a San Francisco engineer named Andrew Hallidie saw a horrifying accident on the street. A horse-drawn carriage overturned as it rushed down a steep slope. The accident inspired Hallidie to create a special transportation system for conditions in the city. He designed cable cars that travel at a steady 9 miles (14 km) per hour, uphill and down. Each car clamps onto a moving cable that runs beneath the street. The cable draws the car along.

San Francisco's Lombard Street is often called the "crookedest street in the world."

San Francisco's cable cars went into service in 1874. Most of the cars in use today date back to the nineteenth century. A cable car seats only about 30 people. Many more passengers stand on the outside running board, clinging to poles and handles. Today, the cable cars run on only three routes. Yet they remain a beloved symbol of the city. In 1964, San Francisco's cable cars were declared a national landmark.

"Pamper the passenger" was the slogan of the Bay Area Rapid Transit (BART) when it opened in 1974. BART is a modern subway system with 82 miles (132 km) of tracks. By means of tunnels beneath the bay, BART links San Francisco with Oakland, Berkeley, and other nearby cities. The system is clean and computerized. Tickets are collected and punched by machine. Passengers sit on upholstered seats and pull into well-lit stations with marble walls. Since computers handle so much of

the work, personnel is at a minimum. The trains usually run on time, but strangers have a hard time finding someone to give them directions.

Despite its ups and downs, getting around in San Francisco is easy and fun. Life in this city has some serious drawbacks, however. San Francisco lies squarely in California's earthquake belt. Living here is not for the faint of heart.

Above: Cable cars on a San Francisco street at dusk
Below: Because cable-car seating is limited, many passengers ride on the running boards.

LIVING ON THE EDGE

On October 17, 1989, some 60,000 people sat in San Francisco's Candlestick Park. They waited eagerly for the opening pitch in a World Series game between the San Francisco Giants and the Oakland A's (Athletics). Suddenly, the stands quivered and shook. The lights flickered and went out. From somewhere in the distance came an ominous rumble. The people in the stands recognized the signs. San Francisco was being hit by another earthquake.

For several long seconds, a grim stillness settled over the stadium. At last, people stirred and asked each other worried questions. "Hey, you think that was bad?" one fan shouted. "Just wait till the Giants go to bat!"

The earthquake that shook San Francisco in 1989 was no joking matter. It destroyed 24,000 homes and other buildings in northern California. Sixty-three people lost their lives. Yet San Franciscans reminded themselves that the damage could have been far worse. This was not yet the "Big One."

San Francisco lies between two major fault lines. A fault line is a crack between the vast sections, or plates, that make up the earth's crust. Earthquakes occur when the plates shift and grind over one another. A sudden shift of a few feet can cause a devastating quake.

San Francisco has dozens of minor tremors each year. It has had two major quakes during the twentieth century, in 1906 and 1989. Scientists believe that another disastrous earthquake is inevitable. The only question is: When?

These two cars were trapped on a collapsed section of the Bay Bridge after the October 1989 earthquake.

The 1989 earthquake affected a wide area. This damage occurred in the neighboring city of Santa Cruz.

In the meantime, San Franciscans are preparing for the Big One when it comes. Architects and engineers try to design earthquake-proof buildings. Schools hold regular earthquake drills to teach basic safety strategies. Stay indoors. Keep away from electrical wires. Get under a table or stand in a doorway. Wait for further instructions.

Why do nearly a million people stay in San Francisco, knowing that another earthquake may come at any moment? Somehow, they are willing to take their chances. A few days after the 1989 earthquake, an editorial appeared in the San Francisco *Guardian*. "We live in earthquake country," it stated. "Everybody knows that. It's a choice we've all made, a risk we're all more-or-less willing to accept as part of our lives. We're gambling against fate, and last week our luck ran out."

Taking chances is nothing new to the people of San Francisco. They have been doing it for more than 400 years.

In ancient Greek mythology, the phoenix was a beautiful bird with red feathers. When it grew old, it climbed onto a pile of sticks and set itself ablaze. After the flames died down, a beautiful new phoenix rose from the ashes. The official seal of San Francisco shows a rising phoenix. Like the legendary bird, San Francisco has been destroyed many times by fire. Each time, it has emerged again, stronger and brighter than before.

THE SPANISH FATHERS

On September 17, 1776, a band of 244 settlers from Mexico gathered in a fort at the Golden Gate. The fort, known as the *presidio,* was built of redwood, but would be rebuilt of sun-baked adobe bricks in 1778. The men, women, and children at the fort had just completed a rugged journey up the California coast. Now they cheered as the flag of Spain unfurled in the brisk ocean breeze. It fluttered high and proud above the fort's walls. Cannons roared a salute. The leaders of the expedition, Captain Juan Bautista de Anza and Lieutenant José Moraga, made ringing speeches. They claimed the land around the fort for King Charles III of Spain.

In 1776, Spanish explorer Juan Bautista de Anza claimed the site of San Francisco for Spain.

XII

dess. et Lith. par Choris.

Lith. de Langlumé.

Coiffures de danse des habitans de la Californie.

The Ohlone Indians, who were living in the San Francisco Bay area when the Spaniards came, wore elaborate feathered headdresses.

Some of the newcomers were soldiers and their families. Others were mule drivers and cattle herders. Several members of the party were Roman Catholic priests. Led by Father Francisco Crespi, the priests hoped to convert the Native Americans of the region to Christianity.

Just a few weeks before this flag-raising ceremony in California, a momentous event occurred far across the continent. Thirteen colonies along the Atlantic coast declared their independence from Great Britain. Most Americans think of July 4, 1776, as the birthday of the United States. Yet the colonists at the presidio knew nothing of this faraway happening. They did not think of themselves as Americans. They were loyal subjects of the Spanish king and of the Spanish governor in Mexico City.

Nearly two centuries earlier, in 1595, a Portuguese explorer named Sebastián Cermeño was shipwrecked north of the Golden Gate. He named the region Puerto de San Francisco in honor of Saint Francis of Assisi. Somehow, that name was forgotten by the Spanish settlers at the presidio. They christened their settlement *Parage de la Yerba Buena*, or "Valley of Mint." They named it for the wild mint that grew on the hillsides.

Not far from the presidio, the Spanish colonists built a church called Mission Dolores. With the mission as their base, priests fanned out through the countryside. By 1800, they had baptized some 30,000 American Indians. The Spaniards forced the Indians to give up their traditional way of life. Instead of hunting for game and gathering wild plants, the Indians became settled farmers.

Life was lonely for the Spanish families at Yerba Buena. There were few parties or other entertainments. Visitors were rare. Sometimes months passed with no news from friends and relatives in Mexico. At the presidio, the cannons rusted. Only a handful of soldiers remained to defend the settlement.

Mission Delores, built in 1782, is the oldest building in San Francisco.

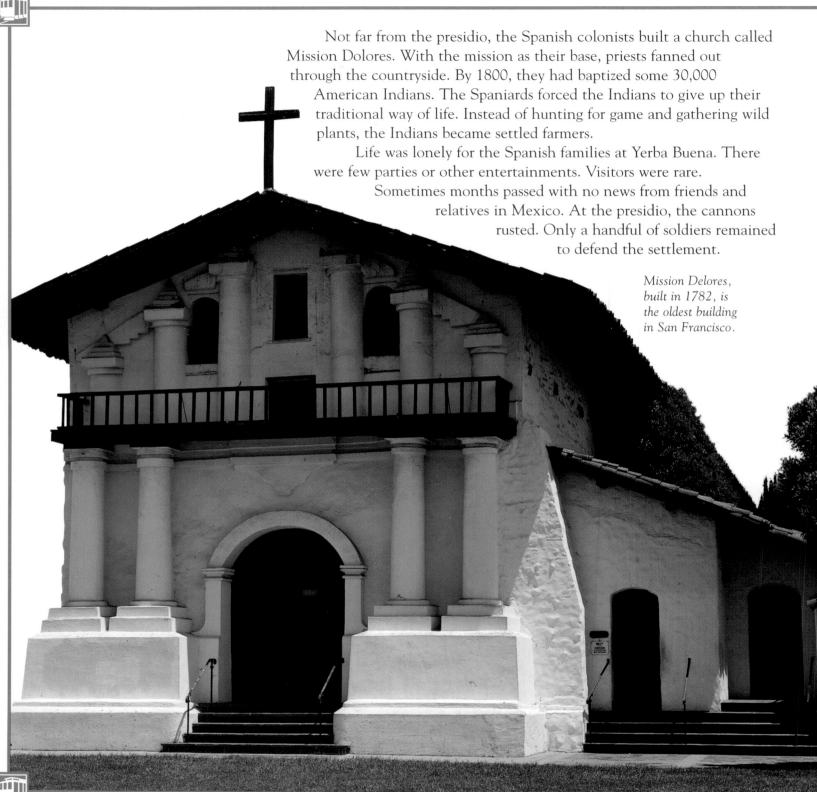

Meanwhile, the United States of America was eager to expand its borders. Americans wanted their nation to spread from the Atlantic to the Pacific. In 1848, the United States defeated Mexico in a war over territory. The United States gained a vast tract of land stretching from Texas to California. Suddenly, Yerba Buena was in American hands. The Americans renamed Yerba Buena. They chose a name that had been used more than 200 years before—San Francisco.

An old photograph of San Francisco Street overlooking the bay

Emperor Norton

In 1859, a San Francisco businessman named Joshua Abraham Norton lost his fortune. The stress caused him to lose his reason as well. Suddenly, Norton declared himself Emperor of the United States and Protector of Mexico. Instead of locking him up as a madman, San Franciscans catered to his whims. The finest stores in the city gave him free clothes. The police department let him patrol the streets in his gold-braided imperial uniform. When Emperor Norton died in 1880, 30,000 people attended the royal funeral.

GET RICH QUICK!

O ne day in 1848, a newspaper editor named Sam Brannon galloped into the sleepy village of San Francisco. Brannon shouted extraordinary news. A carpenter named James Marshall had just found gold at John Sutter's mill, about 100 miles (161 km) away. Brannon had seen the gold himself.

People scrambled into the streets. Everyone shouted excited questions. How much gold had been found? Was there more where it came from? Could Brannon show them where to look? Yes, Brannon promised. He would lead them back to Sutter's mill. All he asked in return was a small fee, 10 percent of the gold they collected.

The discovery of gold at John Sutter's mill (right) began the famous gold rush of 1849.

These prospectors, or "forty-niners" as they were called, were on their way to the goldfields.

That very day, Brannon set off at the head of a long, noisy procession. People carried clattering loads of pans, buckets, and shovels. Many toted large sacks, which they hoped to fill with gold nuggets. Surely, this was their chance to get rich.

Within a few weeks, word of the gold strike reached the states to the east. In 1849, thousands of gold seekers poured into California. Some made the long journey across the Rocky Mountains on horseback, by wagon, or even on foot. Others traveled by sea. They sailed around the tip of South America and up the Pacific coast to San Francisco Bay. As soon as they dropped anchor, passengers and crew rushed ashore and headed for the goldfields. By the fall, about 600 ships floated in the harbor, abandoned and forgotten.

When the gold rush began, San Francisco had only about 900 residents. Within two years, the population swelled to a raucous 25,000. Houses couldn't be built fast enough to hold all the newcomers. Hundreds of people pitched tents along the muddy streets until they could move into sturdier homes.

On this page: Gold nuggets

Most of the "forty-niners," as they came to be known, returned from the hills with empty pockets and shattered dreams. A handful of lucky ones made fortunes in nuggets and gold dust. The cleverest of the newcomers found ingenious ways to get rich by selling things to the gold seekers.

For most of the forty-niners, San Francisco was the last stop on the way to the goldfields. The city's shops sold everything they needed for a proper expedition—boots and blankets, pans and kettles, supplies of biscuits, coffee, and dried meat. A businessman named Peter Donahue invested $100 to set up an ironworks for making miners' tools. The business prospered. Within 10 years, Donahue's company became one of the nation's leading producers of iron goods. Levi Strauss was an immigrant from the German province of Bavaria. In San Francisco, Strauss began to sell tents to the gold seekers. Soon, he realized that they needed sturdy all-purpose clothing as well. He began to make canvas pants, their seams reinforced with metal rivets. Strauss's pants were an instant success. In fact, Levis, or jeans, remain popular today all over the world.

The jeans made by Levi Strauss & Company today look very much like the jeans Levi Strauss made for the forty-niners, right down to the metal rivets.

Left: An 1890 photograph of a miner panning for gold in a California stream

Below: On May 10, 1869, the transcontinental railroad was completed.

Thrown together in haste, most San Francisco houses were alarmingly flimsy. An overturned candle or carelessly tossed match could trigger disaster. By 1851, the city had survived six major fires. In 1865 and 1868, earthquakes caused serious damage. After each disaster, San Franciscans cleared the rubble and started anew.

In 1869, the transcontinental railroad was completed. It spanned North America. Train lines linked San Francisco with cities on the East Coast.

Thousands of men from China worked on the railroad. When it was finished, they settled with their families in San Francisco. The businessmen who owned the railroad became immensely wealthy. They built ornate mansions on Nob Hill. Even their stables had marble floors and paintings on the walls.

San Francisco was a wild, rambunctious city. Its people enjoyed theaters, dance halls, and circuses. Thousands of miles from established cities such as New York and Philadel-

phia, San Franciscans forged a distinctive lifestyle. One visitor called San Francisco "the wickedest city in the world outside of Paris."

RISING FROM THE ASHES

The earthquake and fires of 1906 left the entire city of San Francisco in ruins.

At 5:13 A.M. on April 18, 1906, San Franciscans jolted awake in their beds. Chairs and tables slid across floors. Walls cracked and dishes tumbled from shelves.

A woman named Exa Atkins Campbell described her experience in the earthquake of 1906. "The moment I felt the house tremble, I leaped out of bed and rushed out to the front door," she later wrote. "I was sure the house would fall before I got out. It rocked like a ship on rough seas. Streams of people poured into the streets, a mourning, groaning, sobbing, wailing, weeping, and praying crowd. . . . Quiver after quiver followed until it seemed as if the very heart of this old earth was broken and was throbbing and dying away slowly and gently."

The 1906 earthquake was one of the most powerful tremors in recorded history. Hundreds of houses shook to pieces in the one-minute quake and its many aftershocks. The earthquake broke gas lines and toppled cooking stoves. Fires flared all over the city. Because the quake ruptured major water pipes, firefighters were almost helpless. At last, they dynamited buildings in the paths of the many fires so the flames could find nothing more to burn.

The earthquake and the terrible fires left San Francisco in ruins. Some 28,000 homes and businesses were destroyed. More than 600 people perished. San Franciscans did their best to help one another. People brought food and blankets to families camped in city parks. Many took in homeless strangers.

Over the months that followed, money and supplies poured in from all over the country. New buildings sprang up everywhere. Architects designed these structures to withstand future earthquakes. The new buildings were much stronger than the ones that had been destroyed.

In 1915, San Francisco hosted a fair to celebrate the opening of the Panama Canal. The canal cut across the Isthmus of Panama in Central America. It shortened by half the journey from the Atlantic to

San Francisco and other Pacific ports. The Panama Pacific International Exposition gave San Franciscans a chance to show their restored city to the world. Like the phoenix on the city seal, San Francisco had risen from its ashes.

Visitors to the 1915 Panama Pacific International Exposition saw many beautiful buildings, including the Tower of Jewels (top) and the Palace of Fine Arts (below).

Hundreds of sailboats and yachts bob in their slips along San Francisco's Pier 39. The boats belong to wealthy people from all over the Bay Area. The sailing set was stunned in 1990 when a colony of sea lions took up residence on the pier. The sea lions sprawled on the docks, grunting contentedly. If anyone tried to chase them away, they bared their teeth and refused to budge. The city finally passed an ordinance that stated that the sea lions must not be disturbed.

PLAYING GAMES

San Francisco's 3Com Park, formerly known as Candlestick Park, is the windiest ballpark in the world. Spectators in the grandstand have to hang onto their hats and parcels or they will be carried away. During an All-Star baseball game in 1961, a powerful gust blew pitcher Stu Miller right off the mound.

3Com Park is home field for the San Francisco Giants, the city's professional baseball team. The Giants moved to San Francisco from New York in 1958. During its early years, the team had such outstanding players as Willie Mays, Willie McCovey, and Orlando Cepeda. The father-son duo, Bobby Bonds and Barry Bonds, won a loyal following in the 1980s and 1990s.

San Franciscans are avid football fans. They thrill to the rivalry between the San Francisco 49ers and the Oakland Raiders from across the bay. Like the Giants, the 49ers play in 3Com Park. In the 1980s, fabled quarterback Joe Montana led the team to four Super Bowl victories. Jerry Rice, the team's wide receiver, is hailed as one of the greatest players in football history.

Quarterback Joe Montana (number 16) led the San Francisco 49ers to four Super Bowl victories.

Basketball fans in San Francisco follow the Oakland-based Golden State Warriors. Hockey devotees cheer for the San Jose Sharks. Basketball is a popular amateur sport among high-school and junior-high students. Amateur soccer burst onto the scene during the 1980s and 1990s. Today, San Francisco hosts several local soccer leagues.

Some San Franciscans prefer less-strenuous forms of competition. Golden Gate Park, Portsmouth Square, and other parks have tables marked with tile squares for chess and-

checkers. The game of mah-jongg is popular with the city's Chinese population. Mah-jongg is an exciting game that combines strategy and chance. Players use thick tiles made of wood and ivory. Much of the fun comes from betting on the outcome.

Above: Young soccer players at Golden Gate Park
Right and below: Tiles and racks like these are used in mah-jongg, a favorite game among San Francisco's Chinese population.

THE GREAT OUTDOORS

San Francisco is famous for its clinging fog and fierce winds. Nevertheless, the city enjoys a relatively mild climate. Summers are pleasantly cool, and winters rarely bring snow or ice. San Franciscans spend a lot of their leisure time outdoors. They enjoy the city's parks, waterfront, and street life.

Portsmouth Square, Justin Herman Plaza, and even some downtown sidewalks throng with street performers. Mimes, magicians, and jugglers practice their art for delighted spectators. Aspiring actors deliver spirited monologues and comedy routines. Afterward, a hat passes through the crowd. If the audience is pleased with the show, the hat fills quickly with bills and jingling coins.

A good place to enjoy street life is on the Embarcadero. The Embarcadero is a promenade that curves along San Francisco's waterfront. People fish from the piers, swapping tales of the big one that got away. Vigorous swimmers enjoy the icy water at Aquatic Park. Out on the bay, sailboats race before the wind.

Street performers like this costumed clown are a common sight in San Francisco's parks and squares.

Music in the Mist

The sound of foghorns is familiar music to the people of San Francisco. The bellowing horns warn ships of dangerous rocks in the bay. Each horn has a distinctive voice. Some are low and gruff, while others are high and shrill. In 1954, composer William S. Hart wrote a foghorn concerto. The taped sounds of foghorns are part of the musical score.

Wind surfing in San Francisco Bay

37

The ornate Victorian Conservatory of Flowers in San Francisco's Golden Gate Park is the oldest building in the park and the oldest public greenhouse in California.

Two frisbee players in Golden Gate Park

San Francisco has dozens of parks and plazas. These green spaces give it an openness and brightness that are missing in many cities. "Keep Off the Grass" signs hardly exist. The grass is for walking and lying on. It is meant for picnics, kite flying, and games of frisbee.

Golden Gate Park is the city's favorite playground. Sprawling over more than 1,000 acres (405 hectares), it has something for everyone. Bicycle paths and jogging trails wind among gardens and wooded hills. The park offers tennis courts, golf courses, a baseball field, and even a pond for fly fishing. Fenced enclosures house herds of elk and bison. The animals are used to people. With coaxing, they will sometimes take apples from a visitor's hand.

Fly rods and flies (fishing lures) like these are used by people who fish at Golden Gate Park's fly-fishing pond.

THE FINE ARTS

Among the countless attractions in Golden Gate Park are several outstanding art museums. At the Asian Art Museum, visitors can stroll through exhibits of Chinese porcelains, Japanese brush paintings, and carved Indian screens. The M. H. de Young Memorial Museum contains works from many eras and nations. Other exhibits cover the history of California. These museums invite visitors young and old to experience fine works of art from around the world. They are proof of the city's love of art in all its forms.

The M. H. de Young Memorial Museum and the Asian Art Museum in Golden Gate Park

Left: Poet Lawrence Ferlinghetti opened City Lights Bookstore in 1953.

Below: San Francisco artists work in a variety of mediums.

San Francisco is one of the most beautiful cities on earth. No wonder it lures so many painters and sculptors. San Francisco has dozens of galleries where artists display work for sale. Less-established painters set up easels on the sidewalks and do quick portraits of passersby. They sell their work right there on the street.

In 1953, a poet named Lawrence Ferlinghetti opened the City Lights Bookstore in San Francisco's North Beach district. The bookstore sponsored many lectures and poetry readings.

Monday night was "Blabbermouth Night," when anyone was welcome to make a speech. City Lights soon drew writers and artists to San Francisco from all over the country. Tired of middle-class society, they called themselves the Beat Generation. They believed that San Francisco promised freedom and excitement, much as it had promised riches to the gold seekers long before. In his 1957 novel *On the Road*, Jack Kerouac describes a jour-

ney to San Francisco. His main character wants to find people "who never yawn or say a commonplace thing, but burn, burn, burn like fabulous Roman candles exploding like spiders across the stars."

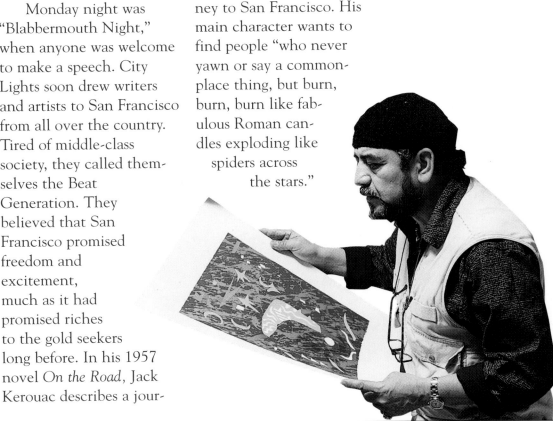

The summer of 1967 brought a fresh wave of newcomers to San Francisco. These young people wore strings of jangling beads and liked to put flowers in their hair. They called themselves hippies and dreamed of a world full of peace and love. San Francisco's Haight-Ashbury section was one of the settings for their open-air party.

Tragically, the summer ended with violence and the widespread sale of hard drugs. But the hippies enriched the popular music scene in San Francisco. The city was home base for such classic sixties groups as the Jefferson Airplane and the Grateful Dead. Rock music still flourishes in San Francisco. When people gather for outdoor concerts in the parks, they remember the Summer of Love.

The Haight-Ashbury section of San Francisco was the center of hippie life during the 1960s.

Devotees of serious music also feel at home in San Francisco. The San Francisco Symphony performs at the Louise Davies Symphony Hall. The San Francisco Opera is based at the War Memorial Opera House. Founded in 1933, the San Francisco Ballet is the oldest permanent ballet company in the United States.

If you can't afford season tickets, you may still be treated to some wonderful concerts in San Francisco. As you walk along a downtown street, the strains of a violin may follow you to the corner. The graceful harmony of a flute duet will catch you off guard as you wait for a BART train. Many aspiring young musicians gain experience by playing on the streets, in the parks, and in the subway stations. Street musicians are among the many surprises that await the visitor who sets out to explore San Francisco.

Tie-dyed shirts like this one were worn by many hippies.

FRANCISCO

Native San Franciscans joke that it's easy to spot visitors to their city. They're the folks with the flabby calf muscles. People who live in San Francisco tend to be in good physical shape. It's probably because they spend so much time climbing hills.

The hills can be a challenge, but San Francisco is a wonderfully walkable city. By exploring on foot, you can discover tiny shops and elegant homes, churches, museums, and hidden neighborhoods. Walking is the best way to get to know San Francisco.

AT WORK AND AT HOME

Earth tremors usually rattle San Francisco several times a year. Because of the risk of earthquakes, the city has few buildings more than 30 stories tall. The Transamerica Pyramid, headquarters of the Trans-America Corporation, is a modernistic triangle 853 feet (260 m) tall. The Bank of America Building, soaring 52 stories into the air, is the tallest building in the city.

Above: The Transamerica Pyramid
Left: City Hall

Montgomery Street is sometimes called the Wall Street of the West. It is the heart of San Francisco's financial district, where brokers sell stocks and bonds. San Francisco is in the Pacific time zone, three hours behind New York City. To keep up with the New York Stock Exchange, the San Francisco Stock Exchange has to open at 6:30 A.M. every day.

A landmark of the financial district is the Sheraton Palace Hotel. Its magnificent glass-covered atrium is adorned with paintings and statues. Wealthy nineteenth-century travelers considered the Palace Hotel to be the only proper place to stay in San Francisco.

Just around the corner from the Palace, the California Historical Society offers an intriguing look at the state's colorful past. Photographs, newspaper clippings, and artifacts tell the story of California from the mission days to the present.

Some of San Francisco's most stylish stores line Market Street. Prices tend to be high, but it is always fun to window-shop. Even the sidewalks on Market Street are attractive. They are paved with bricks instead of the usual concrete.

Above: Market Street is paved with bricks instead of the usual concrete.
Left: A college student of Mexican heritage

Left: This green-tiled gate marks the entrance to San Francisco's Chinatown.

Below: North Beach bakeries sell such Italian delicacies as cannoli.

Centered on Columbus Avenue, North Beach is the heart of San Francisco's Italian section. Bakeries sell cream-filled pastries called cannoli and crusty loaves of Italian bread called *foccacia*. During the 1950s, North Beach lured the poets and artists of the Beat Generation. Today, it still has many bookstores and coffee shops.

The best-known neighborhood in San Francisco is Chinatown. The entrance to Chinatown is the Dragon Gate, which spans Grant Avenue. Among the special sights in Chinatown is Buddha's Universal Church. This house of worship is the largest Buddhist temple in the United States. Heritage walks through Chinatown are arranged by the Chinese Cultural Center. The center's museum displays Asian art and memorabilia from Chinatown's long history.

This arched hallway rises over a row of pews inside Mission Dolores, the oldest surviving structure in San Francisco.

African American culture comes to life in San Francisco's Fillmore District. At Fort Mason, a few blocks away, exhibits at the African American Historical and Cultural Museum focus on African art, history, and music. Displays trace the history and achievements of African Americans in California and throughout the United States.

Visitors catch a glimpse of San Francisco's Spanish past at Mission Dolores. The mission church was founded in 1776 and rebuilt in 1782 after a fire. It is the oldest surviving structure in the city. The building was made entirely without nails. The timbers of the roof are lashed together with strips of rawhide. The walls are made of adobe bricks and stand 4 feet (1 m) thick. So far, they have been earthquake-proof.

SAN FRANCISCO SPECIALTIES

When your feet refuse to tackle the next hill, it's time to hop on a cable car. From the running board, you can get a magnificent view down some of the city's steep, narrow streets. The inner workings of the cable-car system are revealed at the Cable Car Museum Powerhouse and Car Barn. From a platform above, visitors can watch the huge, spinning spools that feed out miles of steel cable. The museum displays scale models of cable cars and shows a film about cable-car history.

Right: Passengers on this cable car on one of San Francisco's many hills have an excellent view of Alcatraz Island.
Below: Coit Tower, on Telegraph Hill

Telegraph Hill is one of the most famous hills in San Francisco. The hill is crowned by the 170-foot (52-m) Coit Tower, a cherished city landmark. Coit Tower was erected in honor of the San Francisco Fire Department. The top of the tower is shaped like the nozzle of a fire hose. On the walls inside are murals painted in the 1930s by Diego Rivera and other artists.

In the slang of the late nineteenth century, a "nob" was a person of wealth and power. Before the 1906 earthquake and fire, Nob Hill was adorned with the mansions of the richest families in the city.

Today, those mansions have been replaced by elegant hotels and apartment houses.

The Cliff House is a handsome relic of San Francisco's opulent past. Opened in 1896, Cliff House is now a landmark restaurant perched high above the sea at the Golden Gate. After a long day of climbing hills, it is delightful to stop here for a steaming mug of hot chocolate. A fire crackles on the hearth. Broad picture windows look out on the rocks and crashing waves below.

Above: One of the Diego Rivera murals inside Coit Tower

Little Hitchcock

In 1851, an eight-year-old girl named Lily Hitchcock was rescued from a burning building by Fire Company No. 5. For the rest of her life, she was a loyal supporter of the San Francisco Fire Department. "Little Hitchcock" became an honorary member of the company that saved her life. When she died, Lily Hitchcock Coit left money for a memorial to the city's firefighters. Her bequest built the famous Coit Tower on Telegraph Hill.

ON THE WATERFRONT

Because San Francisco lies at the tip of a peninsula, water is never far away. The ocean and the bay are too cold for most swimmers, but are popular with scuba divers. They are also very much a part of San Francisco life. The Embarcadero is a 5-mile (8-km) drive along the waterfront. A stroll along the Embarcadero takes in some of the most picturesque spots in San Francisco.

San Francisco honors its seafaring history at the National Maritime Museum. Exhibits include carved figureheads, ship models, and hundreds of photos and documents. The six-masted *Balclutha,* which rounded Cape Horn in 1887, rides at anchor. Several other sailing ships are moored nearby at Hyde Street Pier. A first stop for many visitors to San Francisco is Fisherman's Wharf. Fisherman's Wharf is a complex of restaurants, pastry shops, and souvenir stands overlooking the bay. From there, ferryboats make the trip to Alcatraz Island. From 1934 until it closed in 1963, Alcatraz was a high-security federal prison. Officials claimed it was escape-proof. But there are plenty of rumors about convicts who broke free and swam to the mainland.

Ghirardelli Square, near Fisherman's Wharf, and the skyline of San Francisco

Above: This view from Aquatic Park shows the historic ship Balclutha, anchored at Hyde Street Pier, with Alcatraz Island in the background.
Below: Strollers on Fisherman's Wharf, one of San Francisco's most popular tourist attractions

Not far from Fisherman's Wharf is Ghirardelli Square, famous for the chocolate company's hot-fudge sundaes. The square, with several levels of shops, a fountain, and outdoor museums, is built near the site of an old red-brick factory that still makes candy and other chocolate concoctions. Today, the area is still sometimes called the Chocolate Factory.

Golden Gate Park faces the Pacific shore and stretches 3 miles (5 km), almost to the skyscrapers of downtown. The park was inspired by one man, a Scottish architect named John McLaren. Most people scoffed in 1870 when McLaren decided to turn a wasteland of sand dunes into a park. "Uncle John," as San Franciscans came to call him, devoted his life to the project. He was involved with the park for more than 70 years, until he died in 1943.

Above: Famous Ghirardelli chocolates
Right: Visitors resting and strolling at Ghirardelli Square's centerpiece fountain

Right: The Japanese Tea Garden in Golden Gate Park

Below: Guides at Fort Point National Historic Site show visitors how cannons were fired during the Civil War.

Today, Golden Gate Park is one of San Francisco's chief attractions. Its landscaped gardens contain plants and trees from around the world. A grove of California redwoods, still small but growing, was planted by McLaren himself in 1927. In addition to its tennis courts, baseball field, and golf course, the park has an aquarium, a planetarium, and a Japanese tea garden. Cyclists pedal along 7 miles (11 km) of bike trails.

The presidio was the Spanish fortress built by de Anza and Moraga in 1776. Fort Point rose on the same spot in 1861 to defend San Francisco during the Civil War. Today, the fort is a national historic site. Guides show visitors how cannon were loaded and fired during the Civil War era.

Fort Point stands beside the south tower of the Golden Gate Bridge, San Francisco's most cherished landmark. Beside the bridge's traffic lanes are walkways for pedestrians. The walkways afford a splendid view of San Francisco. On misty mornings, the city waits at the Golden Gate to be discovered once more.

FAMOUS LANDMARKS

The San Francisco Museum of Modern Art

Above: Coit Tower
Right: The Palace of the Legion of Honor

Coit Tower

This tower was built as a memorial to San Francisco's firefighters. It stands 170 feet (52 m) high atop Telegraph Hill. The top of the tower is shaped like the nozzle of a fire hose.

Fisherman's Wharf

Fisherman's Wharf is a complex of shops and restaurants overlooking San Francisco Bay. Hundreds of boats moored here in the years when San Francisco had an active fishing fleet.

Golden Gate Park

Covering more than 1,000 acres (405 hectares), this is the largest city park in San Francisco. It stretches for 3 miles (5 km) from the Pacific shore to the heart of downtown. The park contains hiking trails, tennis courts, a golf course, a baseball field, a fly-fishing pond, gardens, and several museums.

Golden Gate National Recreation Area

This natural area includes parts of San Francisco and Marin County across the bay. It contains wildlife sanctuaries and unspoiled seashore. The headquarters at Fort Mason has art galleries and a concert hall.

Mission Dolores

This Spanish church is the oldest building in San Francisco. Constructed in 1782, the building has adobe walls 4 feet (1 m) thick. On the grounds of the mission church is a small museum displaying artifacts from the era when California belonged to Spain.

California Historical Society

This museum traces the history of California from the days of the Spanish missions to the twentieth century. Displays include early paintings and photographs, furniture, crafts, and newspaper clippings.

Museum of Modern Art

Opened in 1995, this museum is the newest major addition to San Francisco's cultural scene. Some of the paintings and sculptures in its galleries challenge our sense of reality. All of them stretch the imagination.

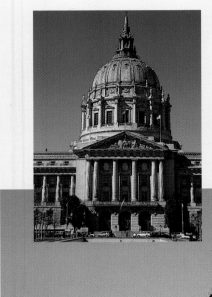

Left: City Hall
Below: Alcatraz Island
Right: The M. H. de Young
Memorial Museum and the
Asian Art Museum

Civic Center

A downtown landmark, the Civic Center is a complex of eight elegant public buildings. Among them is City Hall, built for the Panama Pacific Exposition in 1915. Another attraction is the Performing Arts Center, which includes the Louise Davies Symphony Hall, the War Memorial Opera House, and the Herbst Theater.

Fort Point National Historic Site

This 1861 brick fort was built on the site of the presidio, the original fort used by the Spanish colonists. Fort Point was constructed during the Civil War to defend San Francisco from the Confederate army. Its cannons were only fired once—by accident.

Golden Gate Bridge

This graceful bridge across the Golden Gate is San Francisco's most photographed landmark. Completed in 1937, it is one of the longest suspension bridges in the world.

Asian Art Museum

This is one of several museums within Golden Gate Park. Exhibits feature works from China, India, Japan, Southeast Asia, and the Near East.

Palace of the Legion of Honor

This museum concentrates on European art. Exhibits include Dutch, French, Spanish, and Italian masters from the Renaissance to the twentieth century. The museum has an outstanding collection of work by French sculptor Auguste Rodin.

Alcatraz Island

Lying 1.5 miles (2.4 km) from shore, this island served as a maximum-security federal prison from 1934 to 1963. Prisoners referred to the island as "The Rock." Today, visitors can tour the main cell block and even try sitting in the electric chair—now safely unplugged.

Lake Merced

This small spring-fed lake lies in southwest San Francisco not far from the city zoo. The lake is a pleasant spot for fishing, boating, and summer picnics.

FAST FACTS

POPULATION

City	723,959
Metropolitan Area	1,603,678

AREA 46 square miles (119 km^2)

LOCATION San Francisco is located in northern California at the tip of a long peninsula. The Pacific Ocean lies to the west. To the east is San Francisco Bay. To the north, a narrow channel called the Golden Gate joins the bay to the ocean.

CLIMATE San Francisco has a mild climate. The average temperature in January is 50 degrees Fahrenheit (10 degrees Celsius). Summers are relatively cool. The average July temperature is 59 degrees Fahrenheit (15 degrees Celsius). San Francisco has many foggy days and is noted for its strong winds.

ECONOMY San Francisco is the major financial center of the western United States. It is the headquarters of the Bank of America and the Wells Fargo Bank, two of the biggest banks in the nation. Tourism is one of the city's major industries. San Francisco factories produce processed foods, electrical equipment, metal products, and printed materials.

CHRONOLOGY

1595
Sebastian Cermeño claims an area along the coast of present-day California for Spain; he names the region Puerto de San Francisco.

1776
Juan Bautista de Anza and José Moraga establish a settlement called Yerba Buena on the tip of the peninsula between the Pacific Ocean and San Francisco Bay.

1844
William Hinkley, the first American to settle in Yerba Buena, is elected mayor.

1846
John Montgomery annexes Yerba Buena to the United States during the Mexican-American War.

1847
Yerba Buena is officially renamed San Francisco.

1848
Gold is discovered at John Sutter's mill.

1849
Thousands of people arrive in San Francisco to set off on gold-seeking expeditions.

1850
Levi Strauss begins supplying canvas pants to gold miners.

1852
The Wells Fargo Company begins to carry mail from San Francisco to New York.

1861
Fort Point is built on the site of the old Spanish fort called the presidio.

1869
The transcontinental railroad is completed, linking San Francisco with cities on the East Coast.

1872
John McLaren begins work on Golden Gate Park.

Victorian houses in Alamo Square with the city skyline in the background

1874
Andrew S. Hallidie starts San Francisco's first cable-car line.

1906
San Francisco is devastated by a major earthquake; fires burn in the city for three days.

1915
San Francisco hosts the Panama Pacific International Exposition to celebrate its rebuilding after the earthquake.

1936
The 3.5-mile (5.6-km) San Francisco-Oakland Bay Bridge opens.

1937
The Golden Gate Bridge is completed.

1945
An international conference is held at the War Memorial Opera House to draft the charter for the United Nations (UN)

1953
City Lights Bookstore in North Beach becomes a center for the poets and artists of the Beat Generation.

1960
Candlestick Park opens.

1964
San Francisco's cable cars are declared a national monument.

1967
Young people flock to San Francisco's Haight-Ashbury district for the Summer of Love.

1969–1971
Native American activists occupy Alcatraz Island, former site of a notorious federal prison.

1974
The Bay Area Rapid Transit system (BART) opens.

1989
San Francisco is struck by an earthquake that kills 63 people and leaves thousands homeless.

SAN FRANCISCO

A map of San Francisco with grid coordinates A–K horizontally and 1–6 vertically, showing labeled locations including Golden Gate Bridge, Pacific Ocean, Fort Point National Historic Site, Golden Gate National Recreation Area, Exploratorium, Mexican Museum, Fort Mason, Hyde Street Pier, Aquatic Park, Fisherman's Wharf, San Francisco bay, Ghirardelli Square, Coit Tower Telegraph Hill, NORTH BEACH, Lombard Street, National Maritime Museum, Chinese Cultural Center, Transamerica Pyramid, CHINATOWN, Cable Car Museum Powerhouse and Car Barn, Justin Herman Plaza, California Palace of the Legion of Honor, Portsmouth Square, NOB HILL, Bank of America Building, Embarcadero, Cliff House, Japantown, Sheraton Palace Hotel, TENDERLOIN DISTRICT, California Historical Society, Museum of Modern Art, M. H. deYoung Memorial Museum, War Memorial Opera House, Civic Center, HAIGHT-ASHBURY DISTRICT, Golden Gate Park, Asian Art Museum, California Academy of Sciences, Louise Davies Symphony Hall, FILLMORE DISTRICT, Market Street, MISSION DISTRICT, Mission Dolores.

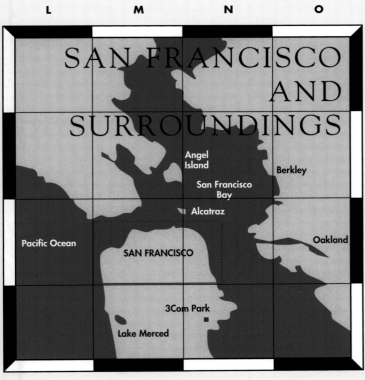

GLOSSARY

adobe: Clay used for making sun-dried bricks

balustrade: Decorative railing

character: Written symbol in Chinese that represents a word or syllable

defy: Go against, prove wrong

enclave: Small, secluded group

exquisite: Delicately beautiful

extravaganza: Highly elaborate festive occasion

gaudy: Overly fancy, too colorful

opponent: Person who takes a different side or viewpoint

opulent: Luxurious

ornate: Elaborate, highly decorated

pagoda: Traditional Chinese building with upturned eaves

promenade: Wide street for walking and sightseeing

refuge: Escape

Renaissance: Historical period in Europe from about A.D. 1400 to about 1600

Picture Identifications

Cover: The Golden Gate Bridge, a Hispanic American boy, a man cooking crabs on Fisherman's Wharf
Page 1: Children at a preschool day-care center
Pages 4-5: The Golden Gate Bridge with mist below
Pages 8-9: A Hispanic mural in the Mission District
Pages 20-21: The business center of San Francisco showing the destruction caused by the 1906 earthquake
Pages 32-33: Fishing boats at the Hyde Street Pier
Pages 44-45: Cars parked on Lombard Street

NDEX

TO FIND OUT MORE

BOOKS

Doherty, Craig A. *The Golden Gate Bridge*. Woodbridge, Conn.: Blackbirch Press, 1995.

Dudman, John. *San Francisco Earthquake*. New York: Franklin Watts, 1988.

Haddock, Patricia. *San Francisco: A Downtown America Book*. Minneapolis: Dillon, 1989.

— *San Francisco*. New York: Macmillan, 1989.

Loren, Stanley. *San Francisco 49ers*. Mankato, Minn.: Creative Education, 1997.

Savin, Marcia. *The Moon Bridge*. New York: Scholastic, 1992.

Stein, R. Conrad. *California*. America the Beautiful series. Chicago: Childrens Press, 1988.

— *The California Gold Rush*. Cornerstones of Freedom series. Chicago: Childrens Press, 1995.

Wallace, Barbara Brooks. *Peppermints in the Parlor*. New York: Macmillan, 1993.

Wilder, Laura Ingalls. *West from Home: Letters from Laura Ingalls Wilder, San Francisco, 1915*.
   New York: Harper, 1974.

Yep, Laurence. *The Lost Garden*. Julian Messner, 1991.

ONLINE SITES

Alcatraz Island
http://www.nps.gov/alcatraz/
Visit this famous island and learn about its history. Take a virtual tour and drop in on the bookstore.

Art and Museums
http://www.navgtr.com/sfbad/art.html
Links to all kinds of great museums in San Francisco.

Bay Area Elementary Schools
http://sfbay.yahoo.com/Education/K_12/
Elementary_Schools/Public/
Links to the web pages of more than a hundred schools in and around San Francisco—find out what they're doing, and let them know what you're doing.

Exploratorium
http://www.exploratorium.edu/
This hands-on museum for kids also has a hands-on website, where you'll find all kinds of experiments and activities. Hook up with links to many other science-related sites.

Museum of the City of San Francisco
http://www.sfmuseum.org/
Visit this museum and learn about the city's colorful history.

Rough Guide to San Francisco
http://www.hotwired.com/rough/usa/
The best places to eat and sleep, city arts, recreation, entertainment, shopping, and tours of the city and surrounding area.

San Francisco Examiner
http://www.examiner.com/
Get today's news, sports, weather, editorials, just as if you were in San Francisco reading one of the city's newspapers.

San Francisco Giants Virtual Dugout
http://www.sfgiants.com/index.html
Team information, player photos, schedules, San Francisco Giants Magazine, and Fun Page. Visit the library to learn about the team's history. Send a letter to the Giants, join the Kids Club, and more.

San Francisco Online
http://www.sanfranciscoonline.com/index.html
All kinds of information about attractions for kids—plus maps and great photos!

ABOUT THE AUTHOR

Deborah Kent grew up in Little Falls, New Jersey, and received a B.A. in English from Oberlin College. She earned a master's degree from Smith College School for Social Work. After working for four years at the University Settlement House in New York City, she moved to San Miguel de Allende in central Mexico. There she wrote her first young-adult novel, *Belonging*.

Ms. Kent is the author of more than a dozen young-adult novels, as well as numerous nonfiction titles for children. She lives in Chicago with her husband, children's book author R. Conrad Stein, and their daughter Jana.